Talking Pictures

TALKING PICTURES

BY RUDY BURCKHARDT & SIMON PETTET

ZOLAND BOOKS · Cambridge, Massachusetts

Several of these pages first appeared in *Conversations with Rudy Burckhardt About Everything*, published by Annabel Levitt's Vehicle Editions in 1987; our thanks and gratitude to her.

Photographs by Rudy Burckhardt are available at Brooke Alexander Gallery, New York.

First edition published in 1994 by
Zoland Books, Inc.
384 Huron Avenue
Cambridge, MA 02138

10 9 8 7 6 5 4 3 2 1

Printed in Singapore

This book is printed on acid-free paper, and its binding materials have been chosen for strength and durability.

Library of Congress Cataloging-in-Publication Data
Burckhardt, Rudy
   Talking pictures / Rudy Burckhardt & Simon Pettet
   1st ed.
   p.   cm.
   ISBN 0-944072-42-9 (alk. paper)
   1. Portrait photography.   2. Photography, Artistic.
   3. Burckhardt, Rudy   4. Burckhardt, Rudy—Interviews.
   5. Photographers—United States—Interviews   6. Cinematographers—
   United States—Interviews.   I. Pettet, Simon.   II. Title
   TR680.B836   1994
   770' .92—dc20   94—19134
                                                       CIP

To Yvonne, fair, bright, talented and valuable.

Talking Pictures

Simon: Why make art? Why bother?

Rudy: Well, to keep busy. You're awake and alive and you want to do something.

Simon: What is it that you do?

Rudy: Well, filmmaking, that's probably what I'm best at. Filmmaking, I feel I have a little experience with — seeing something and getting it on film.

Basically I like pictures. For me it's pictures. When I'm in a museum I see the pictures on a wall. Very often I don't see the sculpture. Sculpture, I have to concentrate on just to see it.

I remember two-dimensional pictures much better.

Simon: Why is that?

Rudy: Well, they give you a picture of something. They're not the thing itself.

Simon: How does the art come in?

Rudy: You mean art in the sense of craft? Well, the art in filmmaking is to keep the film clean, so your print doesn't look scratched, and to make splices that you can't see. And don't get spots! Sometimes when you close the lens down, like when you take a bright scene with a Bolex, the opening gets so small that little black dust spots come into focus and appear on the film. When the lens is open more, they're so out of focus you don't see them.

I don't know if you know what I'm talking about.

Simon: So you want the image to be clear?

Rudy: Yeah, and making a sequence that people can follow, I think that's part of the craft, that people can follow easily, but with some surprises.

Rudy: In the beginning, I was filming the same things I was taking photos of.

Simon: Like?

Rudy: Like — people moving in the street. But when I film, I don't really know what's going to happen; I don't direct, and that can be a lot of fun. Sometimes something happens that is better than you could ever have imagined.

Simon: Like?

Rudy: I don't know. Someone stepping off a curb maybe,

and then a car going by.

Rudy: Once I was taking photographs of a doorway, and a guy comes up and says, "Have they got an encroachment?"
I didn't even know the meaning of the word at that time.

Simon: What *does* it mean?

Rudy: It means that maybe there's a door that sticks out too much into the sidewalk.
And he thought I was some kind of inspector taking photographs.

Simon: Aren't you always directing in some degree?

Rudy: Well, sometimes you try to make people do something special, and sometimes when you have a good day, you think you can really hypnotize them.

Simon: Yes.

Rudy: I used to call it X-ray vision. Sometimes as a photographer you have that X-ray vision.

Everything looks terrific. Almost everything. You can really take beautiful pictures of everyday things, things that happen every day a million times anywhere. It's not a special accident or special drama. All you have to do is look.

It is true, there is such a thing as real beauty, only
it's only a second that you see it. I mean, real beauty,
in the sense of a fact. Now, there's beauty in art, that
is made, carefully, by a brilliant genius, and there is . . .

But Nature itself, or Life, everything, has these sudden
flashes of beauty, that you do see, if you walk around,
and if you're in a good mood you know. You look up and
say 'oh,' and then it's gone, because something else has
happened. And . . . that's . . . It isn't artifice, it's just
the way things are.

But, of course, you have to have a quick eye. And even if
you have a quick eye, you have to have a quick camera ready.

And Rudy sees so many of them. He sees thousands of them.
I see one or two now and then, so I know what it is
he's been seeing.

And I am at that moment perfectly happy, I don't want anything.
I have no bad feelings, about myself, about other people, about
crime, or history, or anything. I'm just perfectly happy for the
second that I see it.

Simon: Edwin Denby* said this about beauty. What do you think of it?

Rudy: I think that's wonderful. That's Edwin? I think that's great.
There *are* beautiful moments. You couldn't say it better than that.

Simon: So that's how you see beauty, as instantaneous, that moment?

Rudy: Well, it's fleeting, yeah, like he says, it may be momentary but
it leaves an aftereffect that lingers, that lasts a little longer,
maybe lasts for half an hour.

Simon: That's all?

Rudy: A really long time, yeah.

Simon: I thought you could see it all the time.

Rudy: Oh no, never all the time. Some days I don't see it.
And some days I look for it and can't find it.
No, I don't see it very often, just once in a while.

---

* Edwin Denby (1903–1983) poet, dance writer and lifelong friend.

But when you see it, it kind of eliminates everything else. There's no guilt.

I like this thing John Ashbery wrote, "It's rapture that counts, and what little /
There is of it is seldom aboveboard, / That's its nature, / What we take our
cue from."

I think that's great. Of course, it's just a momentary thing, it comes and goes
in the poem, but that really made me happy.

Simon: Let me read you something else Edwin said:

> Well, I learned a lot from Rudy Burckhardt's photographs and movies. I got very interested in them, and the way that you can study them, and learn what the texture of light and air is all about.
>
> I wanted that in my poetry. Nobody really understood the films of Rudy Burckhardt because he was trying to capture that, to make you feel as if you might be able to touch the air and light.

What is he talking about?

Rudy: About my photos I guess.

Maybe it's parallel poetry.

In the fifties, our friends, the poets — Frank O'Hara, John Ashbery, Jimmy Schuyler and Barbara Guest — were writing art reviews for Thomas Hess at *ARTnews*. They wrote these lively pieces. Some people objected. They'd say, "That's not really describing the painting, that's not criticizing the painting." They would start out with the painting and then write about something else, but still keeping the painting in mind.

That's parallel poetry and it's great.

You see, anything can make a composition.
Anybody with a talent for it can make a composition.

Like Alex Katz, he makes these anti-compositions.
For example that painting of Ada, where just a part
of the face comes in from the right and the rest
of the picture is a plain red.

That's an anti-composition, an exploded composition,
but basically it's a composition too, because
it's done consciously.

You don't get composition if you can't see that way.

Some people are very dull and make dull compositions.

See, with photographs, on the same day, if you look around with an open eye,
you can find conventional composition or wild anti-composition,
you can jump from one mode to another.
You can take a photograph like a van Gogh, another like a Mondrian,
another like Franz Kline — all on the same day — if you can see it.

That's why photography is slightly unsatisfactory, because it's too quick,
too instantaneous.

Rudy: Well, to take pictures in New York, it took me about two or three years before I was ready, because it was so overwhelming at first.

Simon: How did you get the proper scale?

Rudy: It took me a long time.
(shows photo *Times Square Building, 1947*) Now see here . . . is the first time that I had the people and the buildings together.
It seemed impossible for a long time.
Look at the size of the buildings. Now look at the size of the people.
The scale is so different.

Simon: So how did you do that?

Rudy: I just took the camera and pointed it in the right direction.

Rudy: As a photographer, you develop an instant vision. You see a situation: it makes a picture. It becomes a habit to see that way. And when you paint, you can't get out of it, that's a handicap.

I see the painting finished, but getting there becomes laborious.
You see, I could never draw well. Drawing, if you don't have a natural gift, you really have to work at it.

Simon: You never could draw?

Rudy: Well, I never worked at it long enough to develop it.
When I was a kid at school, I was good at everything except drawing and singing, I got the worst marks in those two.

Rudy: Quite early on, photography became too quick for me. I started painting.
          I liked the fact of a painting taking time.
          It isn't over in a click like photography.

Simon: Really? Photography is over the moment you've taken the picture?

Rudy: Yeah.

Simon: And the darkroom isn't part of . . .

Rudy: No. Someone else could print the pictures. It's better to print them yourself,
          but the photo is already there. However, when you're putting paint on canvas,
          then it's happening while you paint.
          It took me a long time to realize this.

          I don't think my paintings are really any good.

          Did you get that on tape?

Simon: I certainly did, that's a great quote.
          So how do you make your paintings?

Rudy: Well, sometimes I work from photographs and sometimes I work on the spot.
          My painting is still kind of primitive.

Simon: Are you happy about that?

Rudy: I'm very unhappy about it. I mean, there's a saying, "Once a primitive, always
          a primitive," but I still try to get better.

Simon: Haven't you always had to deal with being underestimated?

Rudy: I was never aware of that.

Simon: John Ashbery calls you a "subterranean monument."

Rudy: That's kind of a nice idea. I don't object to that.
         But, see, maybe there's no such thing as being "underestimated."
         That's just a fiction. Supposing a beautiful girl gives me a big smile.
         That's enough. It can make my day. She's not "underestimating."

Last Saturday or Sunday I went to Queens and that was very strange, very desolate. I mean, that's about as abandoned as it gets. You should go there, take a walk there. There's a gigantic mountain coming to a point, like Fuji, exactly like Fuji, made of some kind of pebbles or something, or maybe poisonous chemicals, it looks kind of whitish, but it's a beautiful mountain, big, very big and . . .

It's all industrial, very spread out, a lot of empty lots. I was filming signs. The signs there started looking funny:

ELECTRICAL MANUFACTURING COMPANY — PERFECTION IS NO ACCIDENT

and this, on a garbage can:

WE REFUSE NO REFUSE

Queens, that's a great place to walk because you get away from everything. It's very quiet and spread out. I would look at railroad tracks and the vast warehouses of Bloomingdale's and Macy's.

It's very easy to get to. The best subway to take is the E or F train, and get off at the very first stop, Ely Avenue, before you get to Queens Plaza,

and then you just walk away from civilization.

Simon: What about New York light? Isn't that something special?

Rudy: No that's a fallacy, it all depends on the weather.
         There isn't one typical light but all kinds.
         Clear blue sky and bright sun in the morning,
         dark grey clouds, maybe a snowstorm, in the afternoon.
         Any kind of light can be dramatic or beautiful.
         You just have to keep your eyes open.

         Imagine, for example, the flashing neon signs of Times Square
         under a full moon.

Simon: What about the pollution?

Rudy: True. Pollution does affect the light considerably.
         Then again, it used to be a lot worse.
         The buildings used to be heated with coal
         and that made for terrible soot.
         Sometimes when you opened the window,
         the soot would come in like snowflakes — black snowflakes!
         It's a little better now, I think, less smog —
         oil makes less smoke.

Well, what I love about New York is that it just grew up wildly. Everyone tried to make a bigger building than the guy before him, there was no design, it just happened.

When I took these photographs, nobody particularly liked them.
Edwin did — he said they were the only photographs he'd seen
with visual interest all over. I showed some to Walker Evans.
He called them precious. At that time the fashion was for
social conscious photography.

I have better audiences now than I did when I was younger.
I believe the young people now are as bright as ever.
I think it's ridiculous when people say, "Oh, the young people today
don't believe in anything anymore, when we were young, we believed
in what we were doing."

Maybe I didn't know that many young people then.
I know a lot more now — I think they're fantastic.

Well, you see, as soon as you go
outside of Switzerland . . .

As soon as you go outside of Switzerland, it begins to look very small, of no importance. It's all in that very small place. While I was a child there, Basel was the whole world, with the rest of Switzerland around it for summer vacations.

I remember when I used to go to the bakery and the girl behind the counter would say, "Oh, Mr. *Burckhardt,* what can I do for you?" I couldn't stand that.

Now if she had been flirting, that would have been alright, but she was just being subservient, because I was from a so-called good family.

Simon: So you were a rebel?

Rudy: No, I didn't have the energy to really rebel,
I didn't have a strong enough temperament.
I was a good boy. I didn't make any trouble

… because I wasn't assertive enough,

so I just had to leave. If I'd been stronger, I could have stayed there and lived my own way, and shocked them a little bit, maybe, but I was too timid and quiet, so I could only do it by leaving.

It happened very slowly, it gradually dawned on me that I wanted to leave.

Simon: Always America?

Rudy: No, I didn't think of America to begin with, I didn't think that big.
In Switzerland at that time
when you wanted to be an artist you went to Paris.

Actually I went to London first and that was a revelation.
My first big city with slums and things out of control.
People asleep on the street. Smell of urine. It was great!

Simon: What was it like in London?

Rudy: Well, I was pretty much alone. I was supposed to be studying medicine,
but I went to school only once.

They had a big amphitheater, like in the Eakins painting (*The Gross Clinic*),
very old and dusty, I didn't know English much, and someone was giving a
lecture and...

I began wandering through the streets of this immense city that seemed to have
no end...

I remember the Tareyton cigarettes advertisement:

There's a beautiful woman in an evening dress,
and her fiancé is sitting opposite, and he's blowing a smoke ring,
and the smoke ring coils around her finger,
just like an engagement ring.

Simon: Sexy?

Rudy: Sexy, yeah, in Switzerland, that was considered poor taste.

In America the words "kitsch" or "bad taste" don't really apply.
It's too small a word. In America things are too big.
You couldn't build a city like New York in good taste.

Simon: What of your illustrious ancestor, Jacob Burckhardt (of Renaissance scholarship fame)?

Rudy: Oh yeah, I read some of his books. My favorite is *The Age of Constantine the Great,* where he debunks early Christian history.
They didn't think much of him in Basel. You know the German proverb—*Ein Prophet gilt nichts in seinem Vaterland*?

Simon: A seer is not appreciated in his own backyard?

Rudy: Yeah, right, I think he became more famous here than in his own country.
My mother used to see him in town when she was a teenager.
He was just the absentminded professor.
My grandmother Burckhardt, who was known for her lively temperament and liked to give parties, invited him to dinner, but he would only come for after-dinner coffee.

Simon: Why was that? Because he was too busy?

Rudy: No, because he didn't like dinner parties—or the company.

Simon: What about your grandfather?

Rudy: Well, my mother's father, he was without blame, without any fault, "*gerecht*," that was the adjective, according to my mother. She didn't expect her husband or her sons to come up to that standard, because he was so...perfect.

He was a general. He practically saved the country from Kaiser Wilhelm in 1914. He was a general in the Swiss army and he was a judge.

I remember him when he was retired.
He lived in a big mansion
and I liked visiting him there.

He was complaining about how useless he'd become

but he used to walk around.

Dream, August 1985

Way down in a basement I find my mother, in a tiny dark room just big enough
for a narrow couch, covered with a pink spread. She looks at me sadly,
asks whether I have obtained that position I talked to her about, as curator
in a small provincial museum maybe somewhere in New Jersey. I say no, I had
deceived her, I had not even gotten anywhere near it, I cry on her shoulder,
convinced I will never have any respectable position anywhere.
My mother is worried for me, more about money than position,
while I suppose there will always be at least enough money
maybe inherited from her?

Simon: What was your mother like?

Rudy: Well, my mother was very resigned. I mean, she loved me, and she was very
nice to me, but she had little confidence that I would ever amount to anything,
but she loved me anyway.

I never liked the idea of family trees, especially since they're sometimes fixed to make them look good.

For example, it doesn't look good if someone is divorced and has two wives, so they didn't put Edith, my first wife, in the tree, as if Yvonne were the mother of both Tom and Jacob, only if you look at the birth dates, she would have been fifteen years old when she had Jacob, so that doesn't look so good either.

Simon: Who draws up the tree? Is there an official recorder?

Rudy: Well, usually it's not even a Burckhardt, but someone who married a Burckhardt . . .

We had a great-uncle and he had a beautiful old house right on the Rhine, a very big mansion, and he had lots of family portraits, and there was one of a very pretty woman, with, oh, a lot of finery, and when you asked, "Who is that?" they would say, "Oh . . . er . . . it's . . ."
But once they told me that this was actually one of the family — she had become the mistress of a prince, a German prince.

Since it was a prince, it was OK.

The grown-ups were allowed to know that, but not the children.

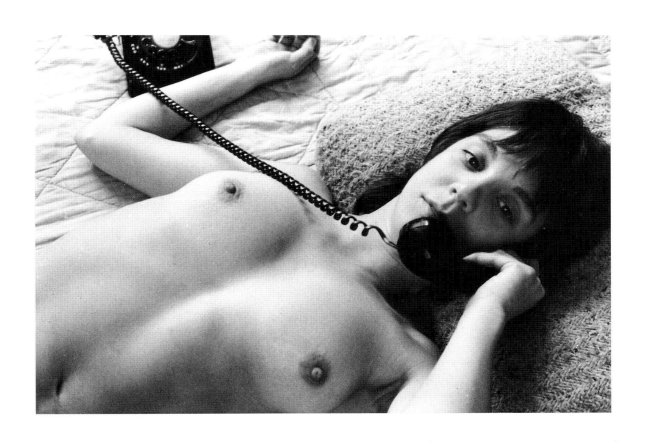

Simon: Any aspects of Swiss culture you admire?

Rudy: Chocolate?

Simon: How about neutrality in global conflict?

Rudy: Neutrality? No, it's just cowardice,
I know that for myself.

I guess I'm just a Swiss dissident.

Dancing in Daily Life

is also seeing the pretty movements and gestures people make. In the Caribbean, for instance, the walk of the Negroes is often miraculous. Both the feminine stroll and the masculine one, each entirely different. In Italy you see another beautiful way of strolling, that of shorter muscles, more complex in their plasticity, with girls deliciously turning their breast very slightly, deliciously pointing their feet. You should see how harmoniously the young men can loll. American men loll quite differently, resting on a peripheral point; Italians loll resting on a more central one. Italians on the street, boys and girls, both have an extraordinary sense of the space they really occupy, and of filling that space harmoniously as they rest or move. Americans occupy a much larger space than their actual bodies do; I mean, to follow the harmony of their movement or of their lolling you have to include a much larger area in space than they are actually occupying. This annoys many Europeans, it annoys their instinct of modesty. But it has a beauty of its own that a few of them appreciate. It has so to speak an intellectual appeal; it has because it refers to an imaginary space, an imaginary volume, not to a real and visible one. Europeans sense the intellectual volume but they fail to see how it is filled by intellectual concepts — so they suppose that the American they see lolling and assuming to himself too much space, more space than he actually needs, is a kind of conqueror, is a kind of non-intellectual or merely material occupying power. In Italy I have watched American sailors, soldiers and tourists all with the same expansive instinct in their movements and their repose, looking like people from another planet among Italians with their self-contained and traditionally centered movements. To me these Americans looked quite uncomfortable, and embarrassed, quite willing to look smaller if they only knew how. Here in New York where everybody expects them to look the way they do, Americans look unselfconscious and modest despite their traditional expansivity of movement. There is room enough. Not because there is actually more — there isn't in New York — but because people expect it, they like it if people move that way. Europeans who arrive here look peculiarly circumspect and tight to us. Foreign sailors on Times Square look completely swamped in the big imaginary masses surging around and over them.

— *Edwin Denby*

And then I met Edwin

And then I met Edwin and that was
just at the right time.

I had studied pre-med for a year in Geneva,
I had been in London and Paris.
I was back home, dropping out of medical school,
I didn't know what I was going to do, I was just moping around.

And Edwin was like a vision of the big world, cosmopolitan and . . .

Simon: You met Edwin where? In Paris?

Rudy: No, in Switzerland. He was visiting with some dancer friends.
        He came to my place to have a passport picture taken, there was
        a thunderstorm outside … oh, it was all very … historic. (I'm kidding!)

Simon: No kidding. When I went to visit Poe's grave in Baltimore, there was
        a thunderstorm. Seriously, was it sunny? Was it dark?

Rudy: I think it was in the afternoon and the weather was mild as usual
        in Basel where it takes a long time to change. Not like in New York
        where it's often sudden changes. The climate of Basel is placid and
        soporific. I had to get away to wake up . . .

Simon: So how did Edwin get you away from Basel?

Rudy: Well, it took a while.
         He was there most of the winter
         and we spent a lot of it together.
         We went to the wrong side of the Rhine.

Simon: The wrong side of the Rhine?

Rudy: Yeah, the poor part, called "Kleinbasel" (Little Basel) —
         the other is Big Basel.
         I showed him a few things
         but he had already found some things
         I didn't know, like one or two gay bars.
         We watched the six-day bicycle race, and that wasn't exactly
         comme il faut.

Simon: No?

Rudy: No, it was lowbrow. Horseback riding would have been
         the right thing to do, but I refused to take lessons.

Simon: Why?

Rudy: Because in those days, in order to be an officer in the Swiss army,
         you had to be able to ride a horse.

Simon: And you didn't want to be an officer?

Rudy: No.

Simon: So in those early days of the relationship how did he present himself?

Rudy: Well, he looked very dashing and cosmopolitan to me. He really knew about everything, which I didn't, outside of Basel.

I remember once he was demonstrating some ballet steps on the street.

Simon: In the middle of the street?

Rudy: Yeah, in Basel, I was quite embarrassed, but I didn't say anything. And I remember we were at a carnival together, Edwin and I. Basel has a big carnival, and for three days anything goes, and I dressed up as a girl.

Simon: You have any pictures of that?

Rudy: No, but since it was carnival it was alright.

Simon: Did you have ribbons in your hair?

Rudy: I think I wore a bonnet and a skirt.

Simon: Wasn't Edwin ever seen as a bad influence?

Rudy: Well, he was gracious and he had very good manners,
when he came to see my mother. I don't know what she
thought of him.

Last time I visited her in an old age home — she was ninety-seven,
two years before she died — we talked, I said,

"Greetings from Edwin Denby."

"What?"

"GREETINGS FROM EDWIN DENBY!"

A smile lit up her face. "Oh, he's the one who abducted you."
That was probably the opinion of all the relatives
though they never said it to my face.

Then Edwin left for New York, and a little later
I turned twenty-one and inherited a large sum
of money from my father who had died when I was fourteen.

So it was really easy for me to get a visa and a
steamship ticket, and join Edwin in New York.

When I arrived in this country in August 1935, at age
twenty-one, I had about $20,000.

That was a lot of money, and I didn't invest it.

I had a letter of credit to a bank here in New York, the Iselin Bank.
My mother's name was Iselin. These were relatives who had emigrated
around 1830 and become very rich and famous; they had yachts, they were
high society. I remember going to this bank with a letter of credit
and I met with Oliver Iselin, a young man with a yellowish complexion,
long thin fingers, pin-striped suit, very haughty, very upper-class.
And here I come just a silly kid. We talked about ten minutes, and I
soon realized, he wasn't interested in me and I wasn't interested in him,
we lived and operated in different worlds.

And so I took the money out of his bank.

Simon: $20,000, that's an amazing amount of money.

Rudy: Well, it was, because this was the Depression.

Simon: How quickly did you spend it?

Rudy: It took me about eight years. I wasn't extravagant.
        Actually, Edwin and I lived quite cheaply. He had only
        a small allowance from his family and for a while
        we both lived mostly on my money, and I remember
        resenting it a little.

Simon: Did you tell him that?

Rudy: Maybe, maybe not.

        But then Edwin got some more money.

Simon: Did you know any rich people? Presumably there were patrons?

Rudy: Well, yeah, we knew some uptown people.

Louise Crane, for example.
She lived with her mother on Fifth Avenue
in a big apartment, huge, with a real Tiepolo
hanging on the wall, and beautiful rugs,
and she invited us (Edwin, Virgil Thomson and I)

and she invited Negro singers to her parties.
I remember Maxine Sullivan looking sensationally beautiful
standing at a piano singing "Loch Lomond."

And Louise Crane used to go around to bars with us
and she always picked up the bill.
But I remember one time she didn't feel like it, she just didn't
pick up the tab,
and we all started reluctantly looking for our wallets.
I could see her point,
why should she always pay for these jerks, you know,
surely they must have *some* money?

I remember my money went down below a thousand and I thought,
Oh my god, what am I going to do now, get a job? What can I do?
I couldn't think of anything, any job, all I thought was, I'm a
photographer, maybe I should work in a camera store, selling cameras?

And then I got drafted into the army and that changed everything.

And then I got drafted into the army and that changed everything.

Nothing terrible happened to me in the army, except getting out, that was an ordeal. I was trying to get out after three years, on nervous disability, which meant I had to make them believe I was crazy. They finally did, and after three months in a mental hospital I was discharged.

They kept me in a mental hospital in Brentwood,
Long Island, for over three months.
We weren't badly treated.
Half the patients were really shell-shocked, but
the other half were like me, they just wanted
to get out of the army.

We had movies in the evening, and once Lenny Bernstein
came and played Rachmaninoff for us on the piano. That
was before he became a conductor.

We played chess and waited to get "boarded," meaning
to get called in front of a board of officers who would
then either give you a discharge or send you back
to duty. I was determined not to let that happen.

One guy who had really been in the war and was shell-shocked
would walk up and down in the dayroom and grunt like a pig
all day long. Another was totally depressed, he stopped
eating. The orderly would tell him, "OK, now eat that,
drink that milk," and he would pick up the glass, and then
he would stop in the middle. "Come on, drink that milk,
drink it," and he would finally.

And then they gave him electric shock treatment and that
turned him around. He became incredibly nervous and
overexcited, and I don't know which was worse.
But it did something. It knocked him to the opposite.

Simon: How did you act?

Rudy: Oh, very depressed. I stopped eating, and I would only drink,
like, one cup of coffee, and have one piece of apple pie a day.
It tasted marvelous! I've loved apple pie ever since.

And I was very convincing apparently. They never accused me of
faking it. It took a while though, it took a while.

First I went on sick call all the time, every day almost.
"I can't go on, I've got a headache, I can't sleep" (I would say)
and they would just give me aspirin,

and then I got a furlough,
they were getting ready for the Normandy invasion,
we were supposed to be shipped overseas,
and I thought, Oh well, we'll just have to see what happens,
and then, at the last moment, there was this telegram,
which said, REPORT IMMEDIATELY FOR EXAMINATION.

Apparently, one doctor, finally,
had looked at all my records, and said,
"That guy's in bad shape, he should be examined by a psychiatrist."
So that's what happened.
And he put me in the hospital for observation,
and I missed my troop transport.

Simon: Perfect.

Rudy: Well, no, not really, I felt very bad about it. It really looked like I was
chickening out, like I was a coward, you know, that I was afraid
to go into the war.

But I just kept saying to myself, "That's not so, I'm not that scared,
I just want to get out of the army."
It certainly looked very bad.

After about three months, I got out.
I got a medical discharge for nervous disability, which means
Very Honorable Discharge.

Simon: Honorably Neurotic?

Rudy: Yeah, and I got all the benefits. There was also something called
a blue discharge, which means Without Honor, it's not *Dis*honorable, but
it's Without Honor.

Simon: Oh, I like that distinction.

Rudy: Dishonorable discharge, that's very bad. You only get that after you've
been in the guardhouse for a while.

THINGS TO SEE

Daily life is wonderfully full of things to see. Not only people's movements, but the objects around them, the shape of the rooms they live in, the ornaments architects make around windows and doors, the peculiar way buildings end in the air, the watertanks, the fantastic differences in heights between adjoining buildings, the fantastic differences in their street facades on the first floor. A French composer who was here said to me, "I had expected the streets of New York to be monotonous, after looking at a map of all those rectangles; but now I see the differences in height between buildings, I find I have never seen streets so diverse one from another." But if you start looking at New York architecture, you will notice not only the sometimes extraordinary delicacy of the window framings, but also the standpipes; the grandiose plaques of granite and marble on ground floors of office buildings, the windowless sidewalks, the careful though senseless marble ornaments. And then the masses, the way the office and factory buildings pile up together in perspective. And under them the drive of traffic, those brilliantly colored trucks with their fanciful lettering, the violent paint on cars, signs, houses, as well as lips. Sunsets turn the repainted houses in cross streets to the flush of live rose petals. And the summer sky of New York, for that matter, is as magnificent as the sky of Venice. Do you see all this? Do you see what a forty or sixty story building looks like from straight below? And do you see how it comes up from the sidewalk as if it intended to go up no more than five stories? Do you see the bluish haze on the city as if you were in a forest? I wouldn't have seen such things if I hadn't seen them first in the photographs of Rudolph Burckhardt. But after seeing them in his photographs, I went out to look if it were true. And it was.

— Edwin Denby

Family and Friends

Dream, August 1985

On the side of Sixth Avenue a wide flight of steps
—like at the Main Post Office—leading up to a
large spread-out building, more like a monument.
Climbing higher to get a better view of the cars
and people milling in the street, I reach the top
of the building, where a big crowd is leaning over,
looking at the scene below. A good vantage point,
I think, going back down to get my movie camera.
But the movement in the street begins looking grey
and drab, the people turning into pigeons, as a
big red truck curves through, narrowly missing
a pigeon that refuses to fly away . . .

Simon: What was your first wife, Edith, like?

Rudy: She was bright, lively, affectionate and had what she called
         "a Mediterranean temperament."

         She came from Offenbach — not the composer — Germany,
         from a well-to-do Jewish family that escaped just in time
         before the war, when she was a teenager,
         and discovering America was an adventure for her.
         We lived together, across the street from Edwin.

         Well, I remember she painted the bookshelves yellow and orange,
         I'd never used bright colors like that before, but I liked it.
         After a while, however, I felt somewhat overwhelmed.
         I felt I had to get away,
         I traveled to Mexico

         but we found out we both still wanted each other
         so we got back together.

         We got married and sailed to Europe to visit my mother.

Simon: How did your mother react?

Rudy: I think she was surprised. I think she was pleased.
         She hadn't expected it.
         We went to Paris and Italy.
         Edith was a great traveler
         with a special affinity for Italy. She's a painter
         and has lived in Rome for a great many years now.

Then Jacob was born. He was a frail, gentle, bright, adorable baby and everybody loved him.

He could crawl so well and fast he didn't find it necessary to walk on two legs for a long time.

Instead of "no" or "more," his first word was "aya" (pointing at a lightbulb). When he wanted me to carry him on my shoulders he would say, "Up papa chair."

When he saw Botticelli's clear and lovely painting of a standing Venus in the Uffizi, he said, "Look, woman nice and clean — no baby,"

and ten years later declared:

"When I grow up there's one thing I know I'm *not* going to be — an artist like everybody else!*

---

* He is, though. He grew up to be an accomplished filmmaker.

Simon: To what degree did you and Edwin live a life of timelessness?

Rudy: Well, in the beginning, Edwin and I would stay up most of the night.
         I remember dawn coming up over Madison Square. Sometimes we didn't
         get up until four in the afternoon, and then I got a little shocked
         because there were only a couple of hours of daylight left.
         But then we went to after-hour clubs in Harlem to watch these
         incredible dancers do the *lindy hop* and the *jitterbug* in the Savoy
         Ballroom.

Simon: What about downtown?

Rudy: Oh yeah. On 21st Street, we used to give parties
         and all sorts of people would attend:
         Aaron Copland, Virgil Thomson, Kurt Weill, Lotte Lenya, Orson Welles . . .

Simon: What about Virgil Thomson? When did you come across him?

Rudy: Oh, he was a very good friend of Edwin's. I think they met
         about 1930 in Berlin where Edwin was dancing in the Wintergarten,
         and Aaron Copland, who became an even better friend, was there too.

         And then, when I came to New York in 1935, Edwin took me to
         these parties, he was pleased to present his "little Swiss friend."

         Virgil was so quick and witty he intimidated me.
         My mouth was usually shut, I had nothing to say,
         but I listened.

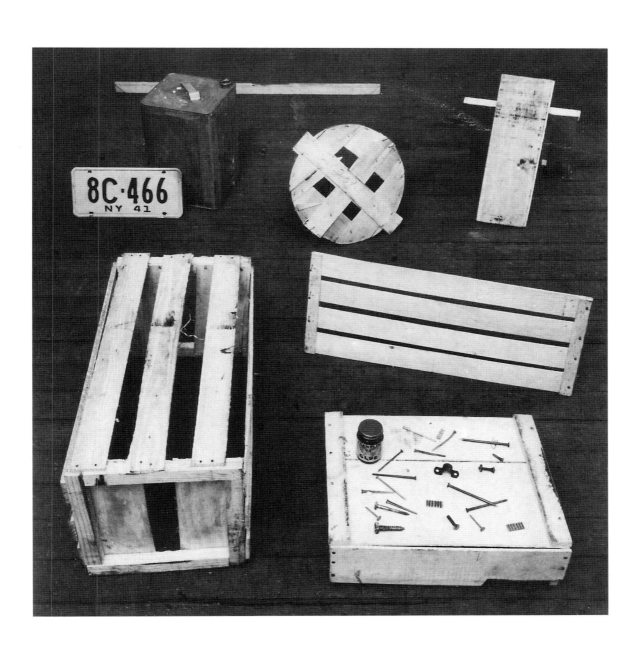

Well, for example, I remember a party after one of Aaron Copland's pieces was played — Aaron was becoming the great American composer, already then, in the thirties, while Virgil was a kind of fly-by-night, a friend of Gertrude Stein, he wasn't taken so seriously.

Once after Aaron had a piece performed, Virgil said,
"Very Jewish music." Obviously, that was a terrible thing to say because Aaron wanted to be a very American composer
— or he said, "I like this piece,
we're getting you down a little bit every year,"
meaning, he wasn't quite as loud as the year before.

Simon: Did he do it to be mean?

Rudy: No, it was just a funny put-down.

Aaron was great, he would just laugh. He was very friendly and easygoing, he had wonderful manners. Beneath it, he was very hardworking in his career. And he was great for other composers, he started the Composers League, he helped a lot of younger composers get performed.

Simon: You were friends with Kurt Weill?

Rudy: Yes, he was a funny guy, everything about him was round:
his face, his eyeglasses, his figure.

I remember once we were leaving a party somewhere, in the East 60's,
some of us were standing on the sidewalk, we didn't know where Edwin
was, and Kurt Weill says, "Where's Edwin? What are we going to do now?"
You see, we needed him to tell us where to go next.

But on the other hand he adjusted very well, and soon he was writing
music for Broadway musicals, and then, later, for Hollywood.

Once, after dinner in a restaurant, he came over to the place on 21st
Street, where Edwin and I lived. As we opened the door, he remarked,
"*Ach, Künstler ohne Geld, das richtige Village!*
Da liegen ja noch die Unterhosen herum!"
(Ah, artists without money! The real Village!
There the underwear is actually left lying around!)
— only it wasn't the Village, it was Chelsea
and we had money
and the underwear, that was just . . .

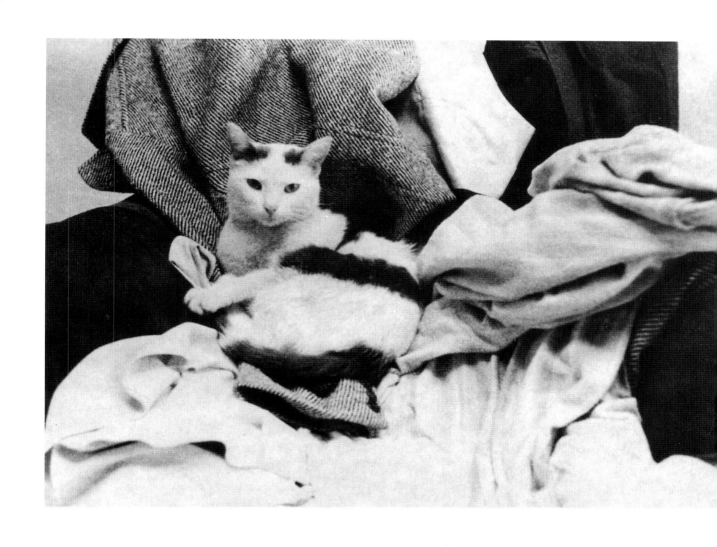

Simon: What about Lotte Lenya?

Rudy: She was married to Kurt Weill, and he was very devoted to her.
         She had a much harder time.

Simon: Why?

Rudy: Because nobody in New York was ready for her style.
         I remember some rich uptown people gave a party for her,
         and she sang some of the songs from *The Threepenny Opera*
         and it fell completely flat. I felt terrible, nobody
         understood it, it was too odd, they weren't ready for
         the Berlin twenties...

         Later Kurt Weill got her a small part in a movie but that
         didn't get noticed either.

         But then, in the fifties, *The Threepenny Opera* was revived
         in New York, in a kind of campy production, different from the
         German one, and Lotte Lenya starred in it, and she did those
         songs exactly the way she had before, and she was an instant big hit!
         And she hadn't gotten better, she'd just gotten a little older,
         but now people were ready for her.

         Who knows, some things may be happening now that people don't get.
         Maybe they'll get them twenty years from now...

In 1937 Edwin and Orson Welles translated and adapted *Le Chapeau de Paille d'Italie,* a nineteenth-century French farce. Virgil Thomson titled it *Horse Eats Hat* and Paul Bowles wrote incidental music. I liked watching rehearsals. Orson was about my age, but what a difference! His contagious, outgoing energy was a marvel to behold. After hours of grueling rehearsal, when everyone was collapsing, Orson would suddenly wake up, laughing madly, and cheerfully rehearse a few more hours. Joseph Cotten played the bridegroom and Orson, the father of the bride. He never liked to play young roles. In *Citizen Kane,* he can hardly wait for Hearst to get old. *Horse Eats Hat* played for about two weeks.* The *Daily News* called it "wacky, utterly wacky, but not wacky enough." Orson went right on to *Dr. Faustus, Julius Caesar* and the Martian landing in New Jersey. He didn't have time for old friends and I remember Edwin's disappointment at being left behind. But that's the way of the theater — "*Die Bretter die die Welt bedeuten*" ("the boards that signify the world").

---

* It became a legend for everybody who saw it.

Simon: What was collaborating with Joseph Cornell like?

Rudy: Interesting. He called me one day and said,
         "Do you want to make a film with me?"
         I knew his work, his boxes. Somebody told him
         I was making films, I guess, though he was never
         interested in my films. It was strictly on his own terms.
         He picked the place where we should start, Union Square
         on a cold, cloudy December afternoon. I brought the camera
         and he brought some rolls of film. Pretty soon I seemed
         to get it the way he wanted it. We looked at the film
         together. Most of the time he was very disappointed.
         "Oh no that's nothing." He could look so sad. But once
         in a while something pleased him and he had this wonderful,
         slow smile. He liked to film birds; starlings, sparrows, swarms of pigeons,
         a lonely seagull in the sky.
         "I'm a sucker for birds," he confided.

A few things happened that were kind of miraculous.
I remember a sunny summer day in Bryant Park.
He wanted to make a sequence about a young girl who had been
at her first ball and had danced all night. Now it was
early in the morning and she came running into the park
carrying a tattered parasol, strangely excited. I knew
someone who had a daughter who was studying ballet, so
she came. We filmed her, a lot of pigeons around the
fountain, old men sitting on benches, people walking by.
Then we both noticed this little girl who was maybe ten
or twelve, wearing a blue dress. She was wandering around
as if completely in a dream. Cornell pointed toward her,
whispering excitedly, I pointed the camera. She never looked
at the camera, never noticed it. He was very happy with that.
We had filmed the other girl, also lost in thought. So he
decided she was thinking about the little girl in blue as
herself when she was younger. One of the final images in the
film (*Nymphlight*, 1957) is the parasol in a trash can.

Art History

Simon: So, Rudy, what about art history and development?

Rudy: Well, sometimes I think it's just a construction that people make up because they can't stand the idea that things just happen moment after moment. They have to make these connections in order to feel more comfortable.

For example, I was around when the artists had "The Club" on Eighth Street. I was a member and went to their talks and parties.

Twenty-five years later this became part of the history of the New York School and people asked, What was the Club like? Do you have any photos? Did the artists communicate there? Did they have camaraderie?

Well, I wasn't aware of it — they had some great New Year's Eve parties — lots of drinking and smoking — there were some arguments.

Who knows, maybe this will be historical too someday, where we're at right now . . .

It's amazing how people feel the need for continuity.
Perhaps it's just that someone has to write a Ph.D. thesis . . .

Simon: You studied painting, right?

Rudy: Yes, after the war. The G. I. Bill was a very nice thing, they not only paid your tuition but even gave you money to live on.

There was nothing to study in photography, and there were no film schools then — so I studied painting.

Simon: You studied with Amédée Ozenfant. What was he like?

Rudy: Oh he was a lot of fun. He was a very articulate guy—crazy, but a lot of fun. He said, "Work with me very hard and in three years I'll make a painter out of you" (I stayed with him only one). "First thing you have to do is get an alarm clock. And don't drink!" (You could smoke — he himself smoked like a chimney — because, at that time, smoking was good for you, it was considered OK.) "It takes three years of getting up early and not drinking."

He was an interesting teacher. He had very strong opinions. He rather liked the careful, somewhat primitive paintings I was doing. The word "sketch" was not allowed to be used; you could make a study, never a sketch. He didn't like abstract painting, he liked Purism — clear simplified forms — he thought Cubism had become too decorative after about 1914. His favorite style was early Egyptian.

I remember after one of the first [Jackson] Pollock shows opened, next day he comes out and says, "I . . . *spiiit* on Pollock." Yeah, he was really angry.

He used to have these uptown ladies who studied with him, but when I was there, because of the G. I. Bill which was a gold mine for him, there were about thirty G. I.'s and only about two or three of the ladies were left.

Simon: What about Hans Hofmann? Was he teaching at that time?

Rudy: Yes. I remember visiting one of his classes. He was going around looking at students' charcoal drawings. There was a model but they were all making abstract lines.

I remember him taking a piece of charcoal in each hand and going right through a student's drawing from bottom to top, saying, "See it opens up the spaces."

One time he liked the way the model was posing and said,
"Stay like dat, I vant to screw you right on de floor"!
The way he pronounced "spontaneous combustion" I leave to your imagination.

No, he was always very inspiring. He made people feel like they could be great painters. Ozenfant always put you down—"If you work hard for three more years, you *might* get to be a good painter."

Simon: How come you never studied with Hofmann?

Rudy: Everyone I knew studied with him, but I guess I wanted to be different. Maybe I should have studied with him, he would have loosened me up a bit; instead I stayed with Ozenfant who was very tight.

Simon: You managed to get word from friends at the Hofmann school as to what was happening there?

Rudy: Oh sure, I knew Larry Rivers and the beautiful Jane Freilicher and Nell Blaine. They all studied with him.

Simon: Tell me about Larry Rivers.

Rudy: Oh, Larry was great. Full of energy, very outgoing and friendly. I remember one of the first times I met him was on a bus going to see a big Matisse show in Philadelphia — the Hofmann students had gotten a bus together and I went along. And then, coming back on the bus, people were kind of drunk and talking and somebody said, "Yeah, that Matisse, his paintings are really empty, you know, they're just comfortable like an armchair, they don't show anything about the poor people, about class struggle, they don't have any content."

So Larry says, "So, well, like what do you expect a painting to do? Stick out its hand and shake your hand?"

We wanted to make a movie comedy together, so he wrote a little script, about shooting up heroin in the john, and vomiting, and all that, but I couldn't see anything very funny about that. I saw him once when he had just shot up, and he looked sick. Otherwise he was himself, intelligent, in control, but he looked all yellow, and I thought, What's the use of that? It doesn't even make you feel good.

So we made a movie — *Mounting Tension* — about Larry being a genius painter and Jane his psychiatrist. We sort of made it up as we went along. It made fun of modern art and psychoanalysis, two pretty sacred subjects at that time.

And I remember Jane said, "Oh, I have this friend, maybe he could be in the movie too?"

So she brought him along and that was John Ashbery, and he played the part of a young man with a baseball bat who hates modern art but gets dragged to the Modern Museum and ends up an abstract painter himself.

Technical proficiency in the best sense of the word is masterpiece painting.

— *Alex Katz*

Simon: What other painters do you feel close to?

Rudy: Before I met Alex Katz, I saw five or six of his paintings in somebody's loft,
small, light-filled landscapes, mostly blue and yellow — no green.
At last, I thought, an American colorist.

Around that time, one of his former teachers at the Cooper Union,
an Abstract Expressionist, looking at Alex's new pictures said,
"But, Alex, that's *French* color."

So Alex started using "synthetic color,"
hot pink and yellow-green,
colors you'd never find in nature,
and started to paint on a much larger scale.

French color — that was a no-no for a New York painter in those days.
If you liked Matisse you had to keep quiet about it.

There was a kind of chauvinism about some of the Abstract Expressionists
which I didn't like.

Some painters were saying, "Oh now everything's happening in New York,
Paris is finished, nothing's happening in Paris,
we're doing it now."

I remember one of them, he got this job to teach in Mississippi
and when he came back, they asked him, "How was it?"
and he said, "I gave them the works."
I thought that was rather ridiculous.

The good painters, like de Kooning or Kline,
they would never talk like that.

I think what's interesting is not that there's this New York School,
but to watch de Kooning's work, how it changes — which has nothing to do
with fashion — sometimes his paintings were quite out of fashion,
and sometimes a lot of young people were taking off from him, it went
back and forth, but in the end, you can see his development.

I found out how Franz Kline painted those big black bands—
I thought maybe he passed by the canvas on roller skates
with a big brush loaded with black paint

—turned out it just looks that way—he actually painted
slowly, deliberately, with small brushes, working from white
into black and from black into white again,
not like calligraphy, where the black is put over a white ground,
all at once.

The best painting often fools you.
It looks like something else.

Like Matisse, his paintings look so clear and direct and fresh,
but he worked on them a long time, often painted the same picture
again and again, until it began to look fresh.

De Kooning's paintings too look like they're done fast,
but they're often not.

He may put down the paint with a fast movement of the wrist,
but then it takes a lot of looking and staring and thinking in between,
before finding out what to do next . . .

And then one time de Kooning said,
"You pick up a brush, get some paint on it, put it down on the canvas,
and you have—fate."

Simon: Fate?

Rudy: Well, he meant "faith," but in the Dutch pronunciation,
it became "fate." I always thought that was wonderful, you know, basically
you don't know what you're doing, what is going to happen.
But you do something, and you have faith,
and maybe it turns out better than you expect.

He once said he wanted to paint like Ingres and Soutine,
both of them, at the same time. Quite impossible but
it was something that could keep him busy for his whole career
because you can't really do it, but you can always go on trying.

Simon: How did you get to know de Kooning?

Rudy: Well, we were neighbors for a long time, first next door and then
         one block away — that's how we got to know him.

         He had some records and was one of the first people who had a very
         good phonograph, which he would play very loud

         (there was no hi-fi then, there were no record players
         that had any good sound, but he had a friend who
         set one up for him).

         I remember he used to play flamenco singing very loud
         and then another record he had was
         Symphony of Psalms by Stravinsky, a very beautiful choral,
         he would play it, you would hear it
         from next door, it sounded great.

         One day there was a little cat that was on the fire escape. It just
         came in. It was a black cat with a little white neck. It came in and
         started to live with us (Edwin and me). A few days later, it turns out
         it was Bill de Kooning's cat, that had wandered over the roof and
         down the fire escape.
         He came down and picked it up.
         That's how we first met — we had his cat.

         And then we used to see him a lot. He used to talk a lot,
         mostly to Edwin, about Picasso, about painting.
         He was very restless, he walked all over the city streets,
         to the Battery and back, late at night,
         so yeah, he used to come over and talk.

Did I ever tell you about my lesson from de Kooning? I had one lesson —
He saw some of my paintings, looked at them, and said, "These are nice,
come over sometime and I'll show you a few things." So I went over there,
and I brought a painting that was in progress, which I'd done from a
photograph, it was of buildings in New York, and he said, "I tell you what,
do something else," and he took a piece of wrapping paper and crumpled it up,
and put it near the window where it got light on it, and he said,
"Why don't you paint this, the way the light falls on these different surfaces?"
And I said, "Oh no, I couldn't paint a piece of wrapping paper, I have to
paint something that interests me."
And he said, "OK, if you know what you want to do, keep on doing it."

That was really terrible of me. And he never gave lessons to anybody.
So to offer to teach me was a beautiful gesture.

I remember someone talking about "pure" painting saying, "Mondrian is pure,"
but de Kooning said, "No, Mondrian isn't so pure, he stares at those stripes
and rectangles for months, changing something here and there,
changing the black maybe, make it a little wider, no, that's not pure.
Maybe Léger is pure, as pure as painting can get. He has an idea, puts it all
down, and when it's all there the painting is finished."

Maybe the arm of a woman looks like a toilet seat but who cares,
the painting is done, direct, very direct.

Thomas B. Hess was planning a story, "Jackson Pollock Paints a Picture," for *ARTnews*. So in the early summer of 1950, the painter Robert Goodnough, who was going to be a writer for the occasion, and myself, drove out to Springs, Long Island, in his rattly old car.

Lee Krasner received us graciously, trying to make us comfortable as we sat around in the evening. Jackson, though not unfriendly, hardly said a word. Next morning, he showed us his barn, where a large black-on-white painting was spread out on the floor. He didn't know if it was finished, and he didn't want to pour more paint on it just for the camera and risk ruining it, but he was willing to fake it by kneeling into the picture, pretending to drip paint from a can of black enamel. The photo of this has been reproduced many times to illustrate his method.

As it turned out the painting *was* finished and later exhibited just the way I saw it. When Tom Hess saw my photos he said, "I don't think I can use these. They don't show the various stages of the painting."

Later that summer, Pollock poured a painting on glass with a movie camera underneath for a film (by Hans Namuth) that actually showed it happening. But he felt terrible about it afterwards and had to drink half a bottle of bourbon.

In the spring of 1964 a great deal happened: I turned 50, was divorced, married Yvonne Jacquette from Pittsburgh, PA, our son Thomas was born—all in one month! That summer we rented a small house near a pond in Maine. Edwin, Red [Grooms], Mimi [Gross], Jacob, Thomas (three months), Yvonne and I. We made *Lurk,* the movie, starring Edwin as the mad professor and Red as his creature, based on the original Frankenstein story by Mary Shelley. We all got along easily until the middle of August when the well ran dry and it felt crowded for a while. It was a great summer.

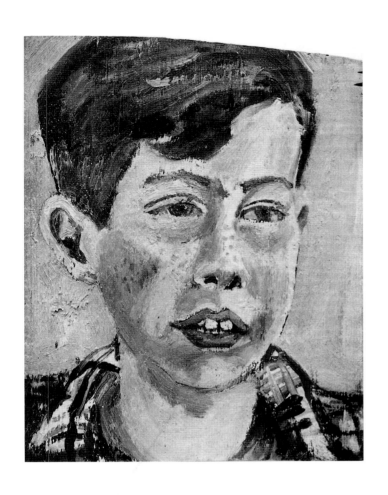

Simon: Red Grooms. What interests you in Red's art?

Rudy: Well, his wonderful energy, the way he goes all out, with no holds barred. At first his work may look wild, just slapped together, but then you find out he's really a perfectionist, in his own way, everything has to have that surreal Red Grooms look, nothing's ever drab or ordinary.

Maybe his best film is *Fat Feet*, about a day in a big city, with sets and costumes and white makeup, totally animated and pixillated, even the live actors in it. He did it one summer in Boston and I had nothing to do with it!

He was very generous and great fun to work with. He and Mimi were an incredibly close-knit team.

I think he liked my more quiet humor and an erotic quality that mixed very well with his own style.

Rudy: We made *Shoot the Moon* with many volunteering friends; it had crowd scenes with over thirty people, cityscapes, moonscapes, three moononauts, moon monsters and a moon wizard. It took us about a year to complete and when we premiered it, a filmmaker-friend says, "Why did you make it?"

The last film of Red's I helped with was *Little Red Riding Hood,* starring his daughter Saskia. We made it in Maine and when the two woodcutters were about to kill the wolf, Red suggested, "Let's make that Albanian animation."

Simon: Albanian animation? What's that?

Rudy: Well, Albania is this wild country where nobody can go. Red had seen it from a beach in Italy, or from a boat, and that gave him the idea: nobody knows what's going on there so their animation is probably quite crude but it might be very funny, and that's what Red likes, he doesn't like things too smooth.

Travel

Simon: They say travel broadens the mind.
I wanted to talk to you about travel. What places have most impressed you?

Rudy: Well, I think the most magical sites I've been to were in Greece;
Delphi nestled in a mountainside, and Delos where Apollo was born
in a cave. Edwin and I were there in 1951, only a year or two after
their civil war had ended. There weren't many tourists and some boys
near the Acropolis threw a few stones at us because we were Americans.

Another truly magical site was the ruins of Machu Picchu in Peru,
on top of a mountain hidden among higher mountains, where the last Inca
Emperor hid out from the Spaniards. They never found him, and the site
was only discovered around 1900 by an archeologist from New Zealand.
Now there's a Hilton Hotel there, but they've managed to keep it hidden.

And then, the Alhambra in Granada, a Moorish palace built entirely for
pleasure. I first saw that when the almond trees were in bloom.
It was still magic when I visited again much later.

Simon: Some people say that you take away a part of the soul when you take a picture.

Rudy: Yeah, in Haiti, Peru and especially Morocco, they think you're putting a spell on them.

In New York nobody seems to care.

However, there's one place where everybody loves having their picture taken — Naples. When you walk through those narrow streets with a camera, children come running, women hold up their babies and girls give you their best smiles: "Take my picture." "Take a picture of my baby." It's like you're giving them something. What a delight for a photographer! Sometimes I wrote down their name and address promising to send them a photo and at that moment I really believed I would, but then I forgot and I'm sure they did too and it didn't matter, the pleasure had been the moment of acting for the camera and making jokes with a foreigner who appreciated their beauty and charm.

In the winter of 1937 Edwin and I went to Port-au-Prince, Haiti,
where I met the beautiful Germaine in a bar. After a while Edwin
left, and Germaine and I moved to a charming pink house next to a cemetery,
with a shower in the backyard, $9 a month.
She was eighteen and I was twenty-three and we were a long long way
from Switzerland.
I wandered around the city and country taking photos and trying to film
a travelogue in 35 millimeter.
Later when I talked to a distributor in New York he immediately asked,
"Is there any voodoo in it?"
"Err…well…not really."
So he wasn't interested.

I was more interested in daily life, neighbors, jokes, gossip, small dramas,
Saturday night dances and ghost stories.
However, after six months or so, it all seemed less exotic.
I didn't want to become an expatriate who starts drinking rum at eleven
in the morning.
I bought a house for Germaine for $350 and I came back to New York.
We corresponded for about a year but then she changed her name
and we lost touch.
I still love to think of her.

Rum and Coca-Cola
Both mother and daughter
workin' for de Yankee dollar
so Mister Roosevelt please call dem home

One day at Fort Benning, Georgia, where I received basic training
with 60,000 other soldiers, there was a notice on the bulletin board:
SIGNAL CORPS PHOTOGRAPHER WANTED FOR TRINIDAD, BRITISH WEST INDIES.
"That's a hellhole, worst climate in the world," some guys mumbled,
but I knew better.

When I arrived there, Pearl Harbor was still three months away and there
was almost nothing to do. I could walk around all day and night
in civilian clothes, make friends, take pictures, drink rum, find girls,
as long as I got back to camp by 5:30 in the morning to shout "Present"
at roll call.

As with most good things it didn't last. After Pearl Harbor we had to wear
uniforms at all times. More and more Americans arrived. They drank too much
rum, they got into fights, and soon downtown became off-limits for us soldiers.

Simon: You spent some time in Morocco, when was that?

Rudy: That must have been in 1955.

[from the Moroccan journal]

TANGIER, MAY 3

Night had fallen and it all was as strange and wild and dirty as I had hoped it would be. On a huge unlit square ragged crouching figures who must have been there all day, were still selling toothpaste, combs, flowers, chopped meat, oranges, dates, handkerchiefs, powdered spices, fried candy and innumerable other things. Women draped in white sheets, or in long grey or black hooded coats, with only their eyes showing above a veil, and hooded men in brown who looked like St. Francis, moved in the feeble but glaring light of acetylene torches. Boys with knitted caps loitered on a corner joking with a barefoot veiled girl.

Tetuán, May 11

In the morning Absalom took me through the same streets we had passed the night before. Brilliant sunlight was reflected from the white-washed walls while covered alleys were in deep black shadow. A column of donkeys loaded with bricks, their leader with a tinkling bell around his neck, squeezed us against a wall. Women with handkerchiefs tied over their faces looked as if they had toothaches. Passing a beggar in a costume of old brown rags, well-dressed men in grey djelavas and red fezes, children in a school sing-songing from the Koran, girls crowding around brightly tiled fountains arguing about whose turn it was to fill her pail. We reached the top of the hill and looked down on a maze of blinding white roofs. Behind the Medina rose the larger, modern, equally white buildings of the Spanish town, and beyond in a bluish haze the mountains on the other side of the valley.

I stood around the square covered with white and black tents . . .
Sacks of grain were being emptied into measures and piled in a heap
on the ground, two men singing out numbers while a third with a broom
swept the stray grain back towards the heap.
A handsome boy in a white burnoose rode back and forth on a bicycle . . .

Simon: Is there any place you still especially want to visit?

Rudy: Well, I'm not so curious anymore about travel. My traveling days
         are pretty much over now.

         Actually, I wish I'd gone to Bali sometime, or Java
         But just recently my son Tom visited there, so . . .

         He's already been to China, Thailand, Burma, Java and Bali,
         places that, back then, seemed too far away, when you had to get there by boat,
         so he does my traveling for me.

Simon: The lure of the new. You must still miss it all.

Rudy: No, you're fooling yourself a lot, you're fooling yourself. That's why
Buddhism is kind of nice. They say you should strive for equanimity.
Don't get euphoric. And don't get totally dejected.
But I hate to give up euphoria altogether, so I'm not a good Buddhist,
just a little on the fringe.

I think that Edwin was really my guru, my root teacher;
I learned a great deal from him without knowing it.

I don't think you have to pay for rapture with pain, I don't think so.
No, it just comes and goes.
I don't think it's something you have to pay a price for,
just don't expect it to last.

Well, you have to get on an even keel.

Simon: The older you get, what does that do? Does it make for any difficulties?

Rudy: Getting old, it has a few advantages actually. You worry less about the future because there's less future to worry about.

You know Goethe said something when he was getting old, he said, "Man often inclines to beauty near the end of his days."

You forget about the problems and the horrors.

And I feel that way actually, now that I'm older,

Might as well look for beauty you know, as the other thing is there obviously.

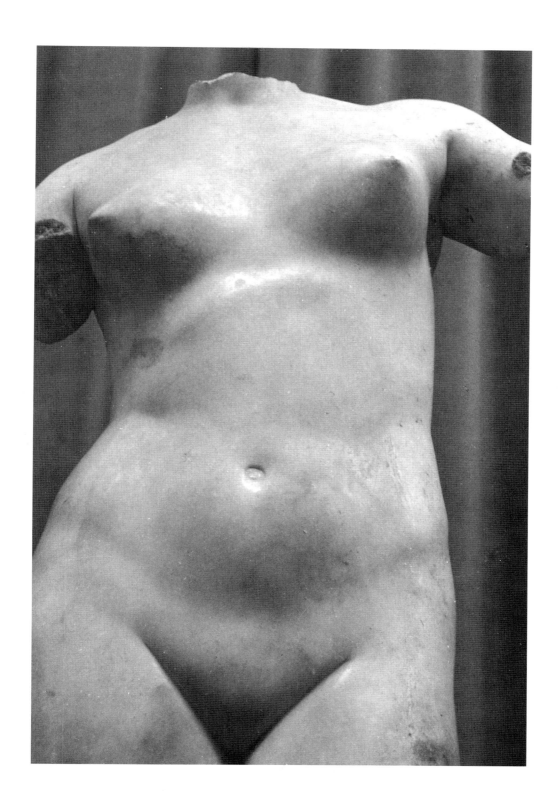

Nudes

Now these are controversial because they're nudes . . . and nobody likes them very much. I've been taking nude photographs for quite a few years and . . . I don't know, some people don't like them.

Rackstraw Downes brought up the word "ogling," and that's a bad word, you're not supposed to be ogling. But I'm not so sure, a little ogling's OK.

And lately I've been hearing the word "voyeur." But what's so wrong with being a voyeur? It means you're a looker, and I do look a lot, at all kinds of things.

"Voyeur" means, I guess, when you're hidden and you look through a little hole or something, but I don't seem to be doing that.

I don't really know exactly what I'm doing, but I like doing it.

"If the nude"— says Professor Alexander*—
"is so treated that it raises in the spectator
ideas or desires appropriate to the material subject,
it is false art, and bad morals."

* Samuel Alexander (1859–1938), *Beauty & Other Forms of Value*

Doesn't everyone like looking at a nude?

Remember, a young woman or man in the street is nothing but a nude with clothes and shoes on. When Botticelli painted one of the first nude figures in the Renaissance he called her Venus or Aphrodite, after the Greek and Roman Goddess of Love. It was a true liberation from the Middle Ages, when a young woman in a picture had to be a Madonna clothed in many-folded drapery. It soon spread to France, Spain, Germany, the Netherlands, but not England or Switzerland. Before long a reaction set in; a fierce monk, Savonarola, took over in Florence and burnt paintings of nudes in the public square. He was burnt himself a few years later, and the struggle between prohibition and the freedom to paint nudes has been going on to the present day.

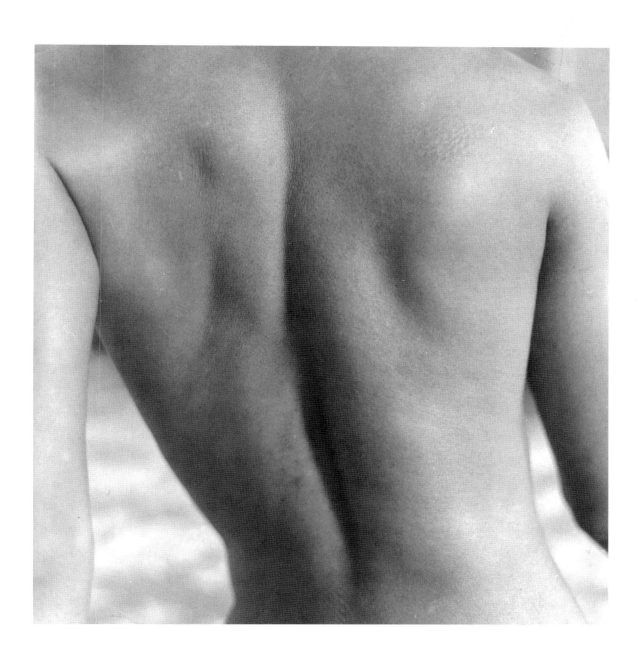

In Rome around 1830, Nathaniel Hawthorne, upon seeing a great many Greek, Roman and Italian statues, thought there was really no call for so much nudity, since one saw only clothed people in daily life all around. In 1890, Thomas Eakins had to put a hideous black mask on the face of a model so she wouldn't be recognized, and then was expelled from the Philadelphia Academy for letting young ladies have a glimpse of a nude male.

However, since the sixties Revolution and Philip Pearlstein's many paintings, our liberation is complete — well almost . . .

There is no right way to look at a nude. A glimpse may be too much, a longer view improper. When in doubt, just close your eyes.

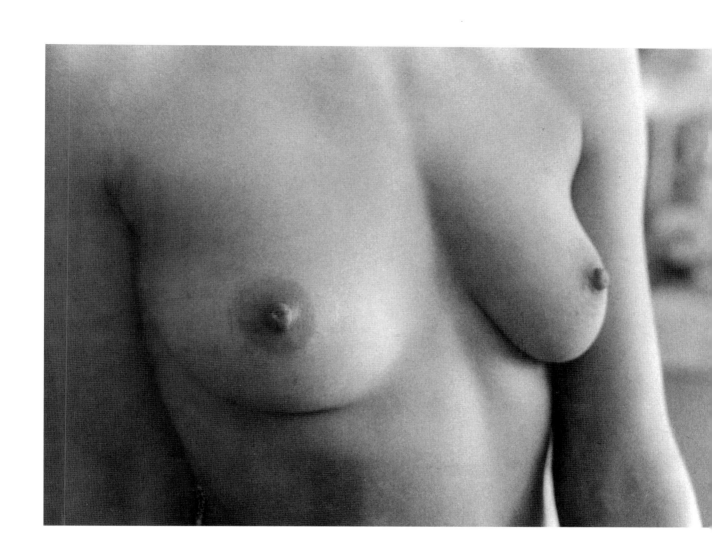

Memory

Yeah, well, so, when I was in that mental hospital, in order to keep my sanity, I'd memorize poems from the Oscar Williams anthology.

So I memorized the part in *Paradise Lost* where Adam is complaining:

O miserable of happy! Is this the end
Of this new glorious world, and me so late
The glory of that glory? who now, become
Accursed of blessed, hide me from the face
Of God, whom to behold was then my height
Of happiness! Yet well, if here would end
The misery; I deserved it, and would bear
My own deservings; but this will not serve.
All that I eat or drink, or shall beget,
Is propagated curse.

That anthology also included a poem of Edwin's.

Simon: Oh really? Which one?

Rudy: *First Warm Days.*

April, up on a twig a leaftuft stands
And heaven lifts a hundred miles mildly
Comes and fondles our faces, playing friends —
Such a one day often concludes coldly —
Then in dark coats in the bare afternoon view
Idle people — we few who that day are —
Stroll in the park aimless and stroll by twos
Easy in the weather of our home star.
And human faces — hardly changed after
Millennia — the separate single face
Placid, it turns toward friendly laughing
Or makes an iridescence, being at peace.
We all are pleased by an air like of loving
Going home quiet in the subway-shoving.

Simon: Rudy, what of death?

Rudy: I remember when my father died,
I was pretty shocked.
He died very suddenly when I was 14 years old.
I was in boy scout camp and got this telegram.

We were sitting at lunch outside and someone hands me a telegram.

That was an event in those days, a telegram.

As I was opening it, one guy calls out,
"Hey, he looks as if his father just died."

I didn't enjoy that too much.

Anyway, so it says, YOUR FATHER'S VERY ILL. COME HOME IMMEDIATELY.

So one of the leaders took me to a train. I went home.
My mother met me at the station. My father had already died
(she didn't say that in the telegram).

There was a lot of confusion in our house, all the getting ready for the
funeral, ordering the announcements, how big the black border should be,
things like that.

And my mother was running around, totally nervous.

That night I fell asleep and I slept very long and very well.
I got completely blanked. And, next morning, the maid says,

"How could you sleep? The day after your father died!"

How could I sleep? You're not supposed to sleep? I got so furious.

You're not supposed to sleep, you're supposed to cry.
And I could never . . . I cried about three times in my life, maybe.

And it was always on silly occasions, like a cowboy movie
(guy riding away in the distance)
when things just seem too beautiful, seem incredibly beautiful,
like a sunset, so incredibly beautiful it would almost make me cry,
almost.

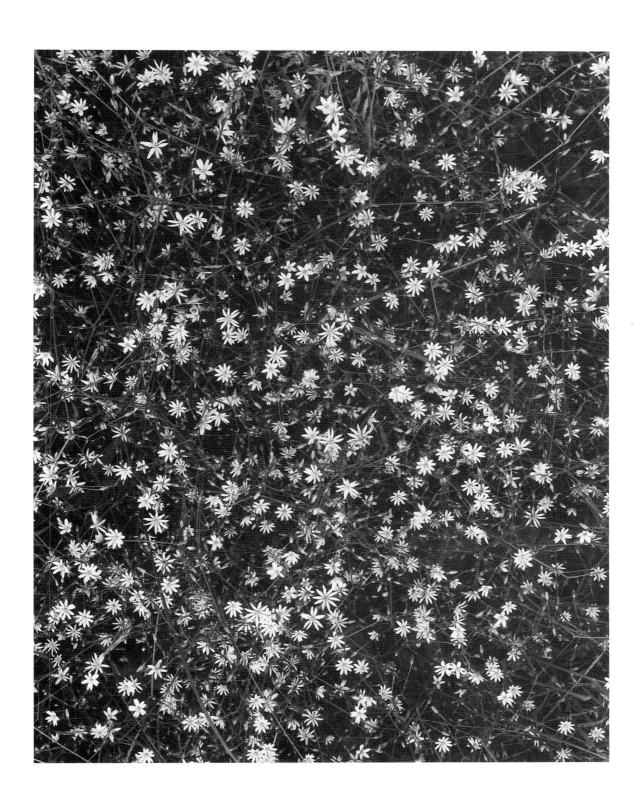

I find that I don't feel what I'm supposed to be feeling
at certain times. I've always been this way. You're supposed to
feel sad when somebody dies and happy when somebody's born.
Things like that. And I usually find that I don't have the right feelings.
I used to think there was something wrong with me.

I sometimes feel good when there's no good reason for it.
There's no good reason for it and I just feel good.

And I shouldn't be feeling good because horrible things are happening?

Well, I was very grateful for that Truffaut film.
Maybe I told you that story?

This young man is working in a newspaper office, and he has an older
friend there, they were very good friends, and the older guy dies.
One day, he just falls down dead (in the office, I think). Anyway
the young man is very upset. He goes to the funeral.
He feels properly sad.

But then, right after the funeral, he lets himself be picked up by
a woman. So, yeah, life goes on, you see?

I was actually very pleased with that story because I too felt that way.

And it turns out that that's a French custom.

Nothing is permanent,
You give up the idea of oh now *I'm fine so the future's
going to be fine.*
You get rid of that.
It's luck. It could end any time,
and you try not to be afraid.

I think it's good you don't know how you're going to end.

Some people are terrified, just terrified of dying, they'll do
anything. Misery, pain, but they hold on to *dear* life.

I don't know,
I'm not going to brag that I've got anything figured out.

Index of Photographs

COLOPHON

Talking Pictures was designed and composed by Scott-Martin Kosofsky at The Philidor Company, Boston. The text typeface is Bodoni Old Face, designed by Gunther-Gerhard Lange for Berthold AG, Berlin. It marks the first time that a latter-day type designer attempted to capture the hand-cut quality of the work of the great *parmigiano,* rather than its classical formality alone. The headings are set in Berliner Grotesk, a *jugendstil* sans-serif, also from the Berthold foundry.

The photographs were scanned by Aurora Graphics, Portsmouth, New Hampshire, which also produced the final film. Mr. Kosofsky retouched the scans.